Bees Help Gardens Grow

Written by Katherine Chu

GRL Consultant, Diane Craig,
Certified Literacy Specialist

Pull Ahead READERS

Lerner Publications ◆ Minneapolis

Note from a GRL Consultant
This Pull Ahead leveled book has been carefully designed for beginning readers. A team of guided reading literacy experts has reviewed and leveled the book to ensure readers pull ahead and experience success.

Lerner Publications
An imprint of Lerner Publishing Group, Inc.
241 First Avenue North
Minneapolis, MN 55401 USA

For reading levels and more information, look up this title at www.lernerbooks.com.

Main body text set in Memphis Pro 24/39
Typeface provided by Linotype.

Photo Acknowledgments
The images in this book are used with the permission of: © Tsekhmister/Shutterstock Images, p. 3; © Lost_in_the_Midwest/Adobe Stock, pp. 4–5, 16 (middle); © diyanadimitrova/Adobe Stock, pp. 6–7; © MakroBetz/Shutterstock Images, pp. 8–9; © kojihirano/Adobe Stock, pp. 10–11, 16 (right); © Przemyslaw Iciak/Adobe Stock, pp. 12–13, 16 (left); © Maria Hoffman/Adobe Stock, pp. 14–15.

Front cover: © Ingo Bartussek/Shutterstock Images

Library of Congress Cataloging-in-Publication Data

Names: Chu, Katherine, author.
Title: Bees help gardens grow / written by Katherine Chu.
Description: Minneapolis : Lerner Publications, [2025] | Series: In the garden (pull ahead readers – nonfiction) | Includes index. | Audience: Ages 4–7 | Audience: Grades K–1 | Summary: "Busy bees are buzzing around the garden! With simple leveled text, this story shows emergent readers how bees help grow gardens through pollination. Pairs with the fiction title Blossom and the Daisies"— Provided by publisher.
Identifiers: LCCN 2024009135 (print) | LCCN 2024009136 (ebook) | ISBN 9798765647738 (lib. bdg.) | ISBN 9798765661956 (pbk.) | ISBN 9798765655351 (epub)
Subjects: LCSH: Bees—Juvenile literature. | Bees—Ecology—Juvenile literature.
Classification: LCC QL565.2 .C45 2025 (print) | LCC QL565.2 (ebook) | DDC 595.79/9—dc23/eng/20240415

LC record available at https://lccn.loc.gov/2024009135
LC ebook record available at https://lccn.loc.gov/2024009136

Manufactured in the United States of America
1 – CG – 12/15/24

Table of Contents

Bees Help
Gardens Grow 4

Did You See It? 16

Index 16

Bees Help Gardens Grow

Bees are insects.

Some bees live in hives.

Queen Bee

Each hive has a queen bee.
She is the biggest bee.

There are many worker bees. They fly from flower to flower.

The bees get pollen from the flowers. They carry pollen on their legs.

The bees take pollen to other flowers. This helps the flowers grow.

Bees are good for gardens!

Did You See It?

flower

hive

pollen

Index

flower, 9, 11, 13
gardens, 4, 15
hive, 5, 7
insects, 5
pollen, 11, 13
queen bee, 7